Reflections on Purpose

Inspiration to find & fulfil your soul's calling on Earth

EMILY GOWOR

www.emilygowor.com

First published in Australia 2022 by Gowor International Publishing

ISBN 978-0-6455734-1-1

Disclaimer

All the information, techniques, skills and concepts contained within this publication are of the nature of general comment only, and are not in any way recommended as individual advice. The intent is to offer a variety of information to provide a wider range of choices now and in the future, recognising that we all have widely diverse circumstances and viewpoints. Should any reader choose to make use of the information herein, this is their decision, and the author and publisher(s) do not assume any responsibilities whatsoever under any conditions or circumstances. The author does not take responsibility for the business, financial, personal or other success, results or fulfilment upon the readers' decision to use this information. It is recommended that the reader obtain their own independent advice.

Dedicated to all who feel lost right now.

The light is there, and it will find you.
Don't give up.

Table of Contents

"The purpose of life is a life of purpose."

Robert Byrne

Introduction

Purpose.

The seemingly illusive and yet all-alluring connection that all human beings seek. The higher truth that answers our existential questions about who we are, what we are here to do, and why we were born.

The doorway to a life of meaning and the invisible force that guides our life journey, even if we are blindly unaware of it. The infinite magic that we cannot see, but that we can feel to the core once we have found it. The pathway to the unconditional love we yearn for and the secret ingredient of all great successes.

It is the Holy Grail: to discover the purpose of our life.

But...

How do we find it? How do we truly know it? And perhaps more importantly, how do we fulfil it?

Being alive and human comes with numerous challenges, of which discovering why you are here on Earth is certainly not the least.

That is what this book is for: to inspire you to find and fulfil the higher purpose of your life.

It is an exploration into all that you are and all that is possible for you. It is a journey into the very core of your being and how a deep and conscious connection with your purpose heals you. It is an inquiry into what moves you, and how doing what you love will transform you. It is a voyage into the magic of the unknown, into what is beyond you, so that you can be awakened to all that is within you.

When I look out at the world around me and I see people struggling, it makes my heart ache. In fact, nothing makes my heart ache more than seeing the potential in people and watching them suffer because they are living a life that doesn't light them up.

This is why I write, and it is why I stay true to *my* path. It is my purpose: to share messages from my heart that may help you discover and follow your calling.

What moves me the most about the significance of what I am about to share with you is that I quite literally don't know where I would be if I had not connected with my own destiny many years ago. In fact, I am not sure that I would be here today to write this book for you.

My purpose has guided me, inspired me, healed me, and awakened me.

It has given me courage in times when I felt weak and saved me in moments when I felt I could not go on any longer. It has single-handedly pulled me through every adversity I have faced, from near-suicidal depression and relationship break-ups to extreme stress and anxiety. It has pushed me to awaken my potential, called me to greater horizons, and brought me to more extraordinary destinations than I ever thought possible when I first discovered it.

It has shown me how to connect with myself, the world around me, and the universe in ways that have humbled me to tears. It has enriched my life every single day and given me the kind of peace that comes from knowing exactly who you are. It has shown me, time and time again, that following the quiet whispers of our heart is how we can rise above that which holds us down, find our wings, and fly.

In discovering my purpose, I found myself. In knowing my purpose, I healed myself. And in pursuing my purpose, I transformed myself. It has brought more miracles – of healing, love, life, and hope – into my life than I can count, and I know that yours will do the same for you.

My greatest wish for you as you read these pages is that you will experience the transformational power of knowing why you are here.

It is that you will catch a lasting glimpse of your destiny on Earth, see yourself as you truly are, and receive the answers that you seek in the process. It is that you will uncover the truth about what isn't working in your life and find the courage to change it.

It is that you will find your unique access to all the strength, inspiration, and persistence you need to thrive, in all the ways that matter to you. It is that you will finally give up being someone you are not, step out of the shadows, and boldly embrace who you are.

This is what you deserve.

May my soul speak to yours on every page of this book, so that you can remember why you came here and make your life the most meaningful and magnificent existence it can be.

"Your purpose in life is to find your purpose and give your whole heart and soul to it."

Buddha

1
What Is Purpose?

Higher meaning. Destiny. Dharma.

All words to describe the same thing: purpose.

But what is purpose truly?

My journey has shown me that the universe we live in is vibrational in nature.

The many complexities of the planet we live on, the solar system, and our human existence including everything you can see, touch, feel, and experience right now, are all vibration in their purest essence.

Your purpose could be described as the vibration – or the frequency – that has been assigned to you as an individual. It is unique to you, no one else has it, and no one else can carry it but you. It is your energetic imprint in this world, in this universe.

With this vibration – your purpose – comes a mission (what you are here to do), a gift to be developed (your talents), and a set of innate desires (what you want for yourself).

Together, these form the threads and themes of your life journey on Earth. Your destiny.

The situations you encounter deepen your purpose, the challenges you meet empower you to fulfil it, and the relationships you engage in are part of it.

Each and every thing you face and feel during your time here is a reminder of this central vibration. They remind you of who you are and why it matters so greatly that you pursue your calling.

Your purposeful vibration is innately connected to your soul. Therefore, you experience your purpose fully when you live consciously in alignment with this vibration; the resonance that exists on the deepest level of your being.

At the core of you, you already know this vibration. You feel it in your heart. You see it in your mind. You are called and drawn towards it. It is your love and light. It is your inspiration. It is you.

It is why you are here: to express that vibration.

And when you do? You will thrive in ways you never knew to be possible.

It never goes away, not even for a split second.

It continually and silently yearns to be expressed, and you will carry and journey with this vibration until the day you draw your final breath.

*"When you walk in purpose,
you collide with destiny."*

Ralph Buchanan

2

You Are Meant To Be Here

With 7.5 billion people living, breathing, and walking on the Earth, it is easy to feel lost; to look out at the world around you and feel that you don't belong, or that your life doesn't matter.

I know that feeling of insignificance well. It followed me through my childhood until I experienced a deep depression in my late teenage years that changed my life forever. I understand how it can be to feel that you are invisible, powerless, or worthless.

But here's the thing:

You are *meant to be here*. No, even more than that, you are *destined* to be here.

You are part of a faultless and flawless universe that unfolds new perfection in every moment. It makes no mistake about who is here on Earth, when and where.

There is no error in your life, no miscalculation of your existence, no disorder about who you are or what you feel drawn to do here.

Your presence is needed. Your love is required. Your gifts are essential. Your message matters. Your actions count. Your mind is important. Your heart is everything.

What for?

To enlighten humanity, to help others, to share inspiration where it is needed, to solve problems, to innovate, to express what is inside your heart, to connect with those who are lonely, to reach out, to collaborate, to evolve, to build, to make an impact, to leave a legacy.

To *live and love fully.*

To *light up* the darkness.

To *be the missing piece*.

To find and fulfil your place on the landscape of humanity, and simultaneously experience meaning so deep that tears run down your face.

To experience the true beauty and depth of life.

Like every human being, you arrived here complete with a purpose that, when fully expressed, would make this complex, beautiful dance of life complete.

There is no mistaking the truth that we all have something infinitely valuable to share.

Your purpose matters.

We can't do it on our own.

"The mystery of human existence lies not in just staying alive, but in finding something to live for."

Fyodor Dostoyevsky

3

The Deep Meaning Of Your Life

No matter what you do, no matter what road you travel down in life, and no matter how far from home you feel you are right now, your purpose is within you. It is ever-present.

It never leaves your side, never betrays you, never wanders away from you, and never abandons you.

Because it *is* you; the vibration that resonates at the core of you.

You don't suddenly lose your purpose because your business failed, because you got divorced, because you lost money, or because your whole life feels like it has fallen apart.

It doesn't disappear in moments when you feel overwhelmed, stuck, afraid, or full of doubts.

You can't mess up so badly or fall so deeply that you become forever disconnected from the higher meaning of your time on Earth.

No matter how difficult your circumstances might be or how great your adversities, the true power and essence of your dharma can never be destroyed. And you don't *ever* become unworthy of your own purpose.

That's not how it works.

Your purpose is your guiding light, from the moment you are conceived to the day you die.

It is inherent, innate, buried deep within you, connected to you.

It is always there, 24 hours a day, underneath the surface of your feelings and thoughts, waiting to guide you to the life you are capable of – and you can always return to it.

No matter what adventures your life has taken you on, you can reconnect with your purpose.

You can pause and look inwardly to rediscover who you are and remember what your life is about – what your life is for.

You can silence the noise on the outside and rest in the quiet knowing of your higher self, of your soul, of your true destiny.

Just close your eyes and take a breath.

It is there.

There you are.

Home.

"Everyone has been made for some particular work and the desire for that work has been put in every heart."

Jalaluddin Rumi

4

A Match Made In Heaven

When this universe assigned your purpose to you – when it aligned you with the unique vibration that would be yours and yours only in this world – it chose carefully.

It would not put the purpose of an athlete inside the body and mind of a scientist, nor the purpose of a dancer inside a businessman, nor the purpose of an artist inside the heart of a race-car driver: unless those were already destined to align (a scientific athlete, a dancing entrepreneur, or an artistic performance driver).

You are *perfect* for your purpose.

On every level – from the hair on your head to the interests you have to those quirks in your personality – you are *perfect*.

It is all meant to be: part of the plan for the divine plan for your life.

You have everything you need within you to fulfil your calling.

Your heart, mind, body, and soul are designed for it.

Every part of you has been carved out especially for it.

And, you already know what to do today to pursue it.

You were born with all the seeds of potential and greatness required to master it, and your life's journey has led you, shaped you, and further prepared you to meet it: to meet your destiny.

Just like every aspect of who I am is perfect for what my heart calls me to do – to write, speak, and inspire – every part of you is by design, no mistake.

You just have to trust yourself, and trust that this intelligent universe you live in, had a grand plan in mind when it chose you for your purpose.

So...

Trust that you are whole and complete,

Trust that nothing is or ever will be missing from you,

Trust that you were chosen for this mission on Earth.

Like hand-in-glove, like soulmates meeting, like stars in the night sky, you and your destiny were made for each other.

"Each of us is born for a purpose, and we want our lives to matter. I don't think it's unique to some of us; it's a longing of every human being."

Garrett Gravesen

5

THE WORLD WITHIN YOU

You cannot truly know your purpose by looking only at the world around you.

It is only through connecting with the world *within you* that the truth will reveal itself. The truth of what inspires you, the truth of why you are here, the truth of your inspiring destiny.

To discover this truth, you must learn to tune out the endless stream of distractions around you, turn down the volume on chaos and drama, and withdraw from the busyness of life so that you can find it.

You must cultivate self-awareness.

Self-awareness is the art of observing yourself in relation to life.

It is the ability to witness yourself as your journey unfolds and to discover your true self and your path forwards. It is a practice of noticing what moves you (and what doesn't) and following your insights to tune in on the central vibration of your purpose.

It is the discipline of putting the puzzle pieces together until you know, see, and feel with certainty exactly *who you are* and *what you were born to do.*

Do not buy into fear on this journey.

Let go of worrying that you might never find it.

Stop thinking it is too late or that you are running out of time.

Give up the habit of comparing your life to anyone else's.

Quit believing that someone else has already done what you dream of doing, or that there is no room on this planet for what you would love to do or create.

Instead, become aware of the sheer magic and beauty of the present moment, for that is where and how you will *know yourself.*

Slow yourself and your life down. Give yourself room to think and feel: to look inwardly and *awaken*.

It is here where you will become still enough to reflect. The ripples on the water's surface will cease and you will *see yourself* clearly.

You will become honest with yourself about what lights you up, about what interests you, about what you care for, and – if you are courageous enough – about what is deep inside your heart.

Remember: no one can tell you what your destiny is. Only you can answer that question, solve that mystery, dig up that treasure.

Is it an easy journey? Not always. But is it a worthy one? Unquestionably.

The truth of your purpose *is* there – deep within you – and it will set you free.

"Anything and everything you have experienced has been purposeful; it has brought you to where you are now."

Iyanla Vanzant

6

Your Life Leaves Clues

You are not in this world alone, nor are you in this on your own when it comes to uncovering your purpose.

In fact, life is constantly trying to show you what you were born to do. It leaves clues and signs, hoping that today you will consciously connect with and remember why you are here.

Each moment of your time here on Earth is attempting to show you what the reason for your time here on Earth *is*.

Every single experience has a message for you.

It offers you a gift to uncover, a piece of the puzzle, or a signpost to follow.

Start to pay attention to the messages you receive; from within you, from around you, from above you. Watch for the moments when your heart and mind are open. Be present to the prophetic visions you receive. These are glimpses of your destiny and of who you could be.

They all point to the clarity you seek.

You have a choice.

You can believe that you are insignificant and that your life has no meaning. Or you can believe with unshakeable conviction that you are *meant* to be here, and that the universe is working with you to fulfil a higher vision.

I know which one leads to the life you want.

Entertain this for a moment:

What if God truly is whispering to you, quietly nudging you to find your path and place here? And what if you truly were born with the potential to make a huge impact, to do work you love, to change lives, to change the world?

It will transform your entire experience of being human, when you embrace that the divine perfection we are surrounded by is always revealing the next layer, the next piece, the next level of your destiny to you: *for* you.

Remember: every day is an opportunity to discover your purpose, and it is right here waiting to be discovered. Every day is a chance to fulfil your purpose, and it is right there within you, waiting to be fulfilled.

We live in a powerful universe, and you are entangled with every single part of it.

Your time here is not random, and at each step of your journey, you are being guided to see exactly what the meaning of your life is.

"Remember that wherever your heart is, there you will find your treasure."

Paulo Coehlo

7

Your Love Lights The Path

Your purpose is not linear or logical.

You cannot *think* your way to clarity about the bigger matters of your life, like what you were born to do. It is not a mathematical equation to be solved or a step-by-step set of instructions to follow.

It is a matter of *feeling*: a matter of spirit and a matter of inner knowing.

Why? Because when you think, you can doubt, question, ruminate, compare, assess, and analyse. But when you feel, you *know*. And the most powerful feeling that guides you to your purpose is *love*.

Therefore, wherever your heart goes and your love flows, that is your purpose.

What you care about so greatly that it makes your heart ache, the calling that moves you beyond question or reason, that which you simply cannot live without, and that which brings your life to life. This is where you find yourself.

Start to observe what you love to do. That is revealing your purpose to you.

Notice what you care about most. That is revealing your purpose to you.

See where you come alive and feel moved from within. That is revealing your purpose to you.

Where do you express your love naturally? What touches your heart the deepest? What are you doing when your thoughts become clear, and your soul speaks? When you live and work from a spiritually transcendent and deeply inspiring place?

Where your love is the strongest, your purpose is the deepest. It is where your true self emerges, when your authenticity shines, and where your work is the greatest.

If you go through your life trying to protect yourself from people and pain, your closed heart will keep everything you dream of at an arm's length.

But the more open your heart, and the freer you are with the raw expression of your deepest love, the clearer your destiny and the fuller your life will be.

Fulfilling your purpose expresses the love that exists inside you, and *that*, is your greatest power.

"The privilege of a lifetime is to become who you truly are."

Carl Jung

8

The Truth of Who You Are

Mother, father, daughter, son, sibling, employee, friend, cousin, grandchild, partner, husband, wife, coach, confidant, mentor, boss.

As human beings, we fulfil many roles in life.

While these bring a depth and diversity to our experience of being alive, sometimes we take on these roles to seek approval, connection, and a sense of belonging.

The desire to be liked, accepted, and embraced can run our lives and lead us away from what fulfils and inspires us deep down: the path of our soul.

Trying to please others at the expense of our heartfelt dreams often leaves us feeling miserable. It is a painful price to pay.

This is why releasing attachment to what others think, say, and feel about you is necessary if you want to fully embrace your *authentic self*, and thus, *know* your purpose.

Doing this may require courage from the deepest part of you. This will be especially true if you have lived your life listening to what other people think you should be and do – and especially if those people are close to you, even your own family.

But it is vital for your fulfilment.

As you let go of who you are not, you simultaneously embrace who you *are*. You discover your *true* role: to live from your heart and soul.

With every lesser identity you no longer try to fulfil, more of your true self shines through. The light of your soul will glow brightly, igniting you from within. Your purpose will become clear, and your life will become divinely inspired.

In my heart of hearts, I am a writer. What brings my life to life is sharing beauty, wisdom, and insight to inspire others.

To fully embrace myself and my destiny – and create the life I love – I had to realise that I would never be a sportsperson, a dancer, a chef, or a singer. I wasn't moved by mathematics, or by science, geography, and history. I had the academic grades to become a doctor or lawyer... but that wasn't what lit up my spirit.

I was called by the artful use of words, to inspire others to live a more meaningful life. When I let go of the everything that I *could* have been, I fell safely and firmly into the life I was born for – and what a life it has been.

I invite you to have the self-love and humility to admit who you are not, and the strength to release any emotional attachment to being a lesser version of who you truly are. Remind yourself that you are here for an all-important reason, and that the greatest gift you can give to this world is to find and fulfil it.

As you release the 'not you', the true you will be waiting with open arms.

Being loved for your authentic self is far greater than being accepted for someone you are not, and by courageously admitting who you are not, you embrace the power and beauty of who you *are*.

And that, is where your purpose lies.

"Let yourself be silently drawn by the strange pull of what you really love. It will not lead you astray."

Rumi

9

You Are A Masterpiece

Every single human being on this planet was born with a purpose.

Every person who walked before you, every person who walks beside you, and every person who will walk after you was not and is not put here by chance.

We each have a unique work to fulfil in this world. Whether it is grand or small in scale and regardless of expression, there is something meaningful and significant for each of us to do in our time here.

No two purposes are ever the same.

Each one – each path, each mission, each vision – is as unique as the person who carries it.

It is for this reason that comparing who you are to *anyone* else is not only futile – because you will inevitably end up coming home to who you are anyway – it is the cause of an unfulfilling existence.

It would be a great misfortune for you, for your future, for your loved ones, for your community, and for the world, if you lived your life so determined to change who you are that you missed out on *being* who you are.

The mere thought that maybe you 'should' try to be more like anyone else distracts you from the infinite potential, ideas, and opportunities that life has in store for you. But when you *love* you, you unlock and unleash what is possible for your future.

Because your purpose is unique to you, your journey to fulfil that purpose is also unique.

The events that shape you, the twists and turns that led you here, the lessons, blessings and gifts on your path, your dream career – they are all specific to *you*. Therefore, neither you nor your path can be compared to any other human being or their journey.

The more you honour and respect your individuality and the unrepeatable and exclusive nature of your journey, the clearer your purpose will become.

The greatest insult you could ever give yourself is to try to be less of who you are and more like someone else.

You are a one-of-a-kind, and you were born with reason, meaning, and potential. No one else can take your place on the stage of life. Your presence here is needed.

So, lean into your purpose.

Lean into who you are, love who you are, and step courageously into what you feel called to do.

"Love takes off masks that we fear we cannot live without and know we cannot live within."

James Baldwin

10

Trust In The Divine Plan For Your Life

Experiencing emotions is part of being human.

Regardless of who you are, where you are, what you do, or what your background is, you will feel them.

Sadness, frustration, resentment, elation, depression, guilt, fear, shame, envy, regret. They will appear in your life and on your journey, at different times, in different extremes, for different reasons; from heartbreak and job loss to personal struggle.

If you hold onto them, they will weigh you down. Your spirit will feel heavy, and your life will feel draining.

If you refuse to let go – or if you exaggerate and exacerbate them – you may eventually become completely closed off, cynical, resistant, stuck, and ignorant to the pure wonder of being alive.

You will lose your life force and perhaps, your will to live. Your emotional wounding will blind you from the love that surrounds you, and your purpose along with it.

This is why releasing bitterness, grief, and any other emotion that drains you is so important. Crucial, even. Why? Because emotional baggage and a full and extraordinary life lived on purpose don't go hand-in-hand.

As you heal your inner wounds – by realising that not a single part of you nor your life has ever been out of place – you peel back the layers of your pain and suffering and discover your authentic self.

In fact, in moments of true healing, all that is left is *YOU* – and what you were born to do.

The drama fades away and the truth remains: the purest essence of what you love to do, your gifts, and what you would love to spend your life pursuing.

Among the many blessings that deep and personal healing can bring – increased wellness, a better quality of life, and many forms of wealth included – this may be the greatest.

That by having the courage to look within and open your heart to love, you can discover not only the profound beauty of life, but the profound beauty of *you*. That by surrendering the pain, layer by layer, you can discover why you are here.

And then, be truly free to fulfil it.

You are not your emotions. You are not your wounds. You are not your past. You are far greater than all of these.

It is time to become one, not with a story of how or why your life has been hard, but rather with the story of what you could accomplish by realising you are born for so much more.

Your purpose is right there, under the surface, waiting to be uncovered, discovered, revealed, and fulfilled by you.

It is life's gift to you.

"Knowing your life purpose is the first step toward living a truly conscious life. A life purpose provides us with a clear goal, a set finish line that you truly want to reach."

Simon Foster

11

In The Silence, There You Are

Life is noisy. The world is noisy. Humanity is noisy. Social media is noisy. The noise of drama, the noise of opinion, the noise of idealisms, the noise of emotions.

The sound of it can be deafening. It can drown out the sound that matters: the song of your soul. Your why. Your heart. Your legacy. Your purpose.

Learning to turn down the volume on the outside world, even for a moment each day, will help to guide you inwards. That pause in the chaos, the precious moments of presence where you tune out the static around you to hear the frequency within you, will become your ally in discovering what your life is truly about.

As the noise around you fades away, the voice within you can be heard... and it speaks, every time you listen.

Although we may sometimes resist doing this – because sitting in the silence can seem a terrifying thing after a life amongst the noise – it is there, in the solitude, that we can think clearly, see clearly, hear clearly, and feel clearly.

In that clarity, there you are.

The real you.

Stunning in simplicity, profound, powerful, radiant, and brilliant.

The big picture of your life. The inspiration you need. The vision for your future that can single-handedly drive you to turn your life around and align it with your calling. The answers you need to move forward.

It is all there, waiting to be discovered in the silence.

So, have the courage to become quiet. To pull back from those around you, from external events, from the chitter-chatter of human life on Earth. To allow the many voices inside your mind to fade into the background. To drop into the void, into the quiet, into the nothingness, into 'God'.

Find that sacred stillness, no matter how loud the sounds around you, or regardless of how busy or chaotic or intense your life may be right now.

Listen to what your inner voice is saying.

It is speaking to you, waiting for you to listen, so that it can whisper to you the secret you've been yearning to hear.

Ask it about your purpose – and wait for the answers.

They will be there.

"Discovering your purpose is the most significant thing you will do in your life. You, your loved ones, and the world will be better off because you went on this journey."

Mastin Kipp

12

The Doorway To Your Purpose

A deep knowing of your purpose requires a deep relationship with who you are.

One of the most powerful ways to expand and strengthen this relationship is to engage in a spiritual practice.

Journaling, meditation, jogging, yoga, walking in nature, dancing, listening to music, cycling, sacred ceremony. They are equally powerful doorways to the temple within.

It doesn't matter so much *what* the practice is. What matters most is that it feels like yours: a place where you can return home spiritually.

Once you find the right one for you, it will be your ally for the rest of your life.

It will support you to discover your strengths, heal your shadows, navigate the many situations you face, and fulfil the most authentic expression of your soul while alive.

It will bless you with infinite riches, pull you up in your darkest hours, and keep you on your path.

Its purpose is to guide you, away from drama and distraction and deeply inward to the very core of your being. Towards *your* purpose.

Every time you show up for your practice, it will reward you.

Some days, your spiritual practice will facilitate healing and enlightenment so deep that tears stream down your face. Other days, you will receive a mere tiny insight that gets you through that day. Both experiences will serve you greatly.

Over time, these glimpses of insight – these flashes of light from within – will add up. Piece by piece, they will form a complete picture: the vision for your future and the central purpose for your life that illuminates it.

Your practice will allow your mind to become quiet, so that your soul can speak.

It will gift you with the precious opportunity to communicate with your higher self and your deepest source of wisdom; your ultimate guide and companion.

It will give the veils of confusion time to fall away so that you can see the truth.

The truth of why you are here and what truly matters in your time on Earth.

"As you open yourself to living at your edge, your deepest purpose will slowly begin to make itself known."

David Deida

13

Commune With Your Higher Self

Ultimately, the discovery of your purpose requires you to connect with your higher self.

Your higher self is the 'you' that observes you, in everything you do. It is your higher mind. It is the illuminated, all-seeing, and wise part of you. It is the voice within. It is your essence. It is the self *beyond* the human self.

That higher self knows you intimately. It is connected to everything that is – God, source, universal intelligence – and it knows with quiet resolution and rock-solid certainty what your divine destiny is.

It sees what lights you up, it knows what kind of life will bring you meaning, and it wants nothing more than for you to thrive in pursuit of what you love most.

Your higher self tries to show you the way, every day. It is constantly guiding you, nudging you, and whispering to you, encouraging you to follow the path that lives inside your heart. It wants to communicate with you and help you succeed. It is *you*.

To connect with it – to connect with the higher *you* – delve deep into your spiritual practice, into the silence, into your own heart, into the space between the words, and be prepared to discover something new with the power to change your future.

It is important to let go of attachments; to release your tight grip on how you think you or your life are meant to be. It is important to set your fears free and cease worrying about whether your time here will add up or if your dreams will work out. It is important to open your heart and love yourself fully.

It is important to believe, without resistance, that the source that created you does have a grand plan in mind for you.

This conviction, together with an undying curiosity to know yourself deeply, will lead you to your destiny. It will help you to find your path and thus, your place, in this big, big world.

Your human self worries, compares, doubts, questions, sees limitations, and tries to 'make it work' and 'figure it out'. But your higher self simply *knows*.

So...

Listen for your soul,

Feel your heart,

And allow it to guide your life.

"We all have a purpose in life, and when you find yours you will recognise it."

Catherine Pulsifer

14

WHEN YOU STRIKE GOLD

You will know you have found your purpose because it will start to transform your life, from the inside out.

Your work will become your life's work,

Your relationships will develop a new depth and meaning,

And even the most ordinary of days will suddenly seem extraordinary.

Everything will start to fall into place.

What didn't make sense will now be as clear as day: where your interests lie, why you are wired the way you are, why you are drawn to certain things.

Where before you couldn't see where to go and which path to take next, you will now be able to see your plans with 20/20 vision. You will know your true identity and be able to get to work building a life that fulfils you.

Moments of conscious connection with what you were born to do will touch your heart, inspire your mind, bring tears to your eyes, and give you goosebumps.

You will feel ignited from within and pulled by a calling far beyond you.

You will rise beyond normal human pursuits – like survival and paying bills – and be drawn to do and achieve something truly worthwhile. Transcendent. Meaningful. Inspiring. Soulful. World-changing.

Life flows differently when we discover our dharma and do what we love. It shines light into your life, from deep within you to the world around you. It is when we live in line with what inspires us most that we feel the most alive.

Above all else, you will know you have found your purpose because it will feel as though you have struck gold.

Because you have discovered the real treasure of being human: the key to a life so fulfilling that you need to pinch yourself.

From lost to found,

From drifting to driven,

From depressed to inspired.

That is the power that becomes unleashed when you connect with the ‘why’ for your life.

"Musicians must make music, artists must paint, poets must write if they are ultimately to be at peace with themselves. What humans can be, they must be."

Abraham Maslow

15

The Extraordinary Life You Deserve

The spark of your purpose is the starting point of a life less ordinary.

It is the seed for your greatness, the key to your achievement, the vision for your wealth, the why for your wellness, the reason for your love and connection.

From there – from this profound clarity on *who you are* and *what you were born to do* – you can begin to chart a new path.

You can find a career that fulfils your heart, discover ways to be paid for your gifts, expand your confidence, build momentum, and change the world with your presence.

It is astounding how everything *around* you comes into crystal clear focus once you have crystal clear focus *within* you.

Your purpose is the blueprint to your future, as well as the compass to navigate your way to greener pastures and new levels... to the future you desire and deserve.

It quells the feeling that you are lost, and provides every signpost and direction you will ever need to make your life here an extraordinary one.

So, don't ignore the dreams inside your heart; they are telling you which way to go. If this means changing tracks or starting over, find the courage to do it. You won't regret it – believe me this.

Allow the energy of your purpose to push, pull, and guide you forwards.

Day by day, establish a new life for yourself: a life that has deep meaning, that inspires you to tears, that fulfils you on every level.

A life that is original and unique to *you*.

A life that is *filled* with everything that has meaning for you.

A life that *inspires* the deepest levels of your being.

A life that brings you to *life*.

That is what you are here for.

Settle for nothing less.

"A person without a purpose is like a ship without a rudder."

Thomas Carlyle

16

Decisions That Alter Your Destiny

Navigating our way through life can be overwhelming and confusing.

At some stage in our journey, we each have a blank canvas ahead of us and we must decide what kind of life we want to create with it.

With this enormous privilege and responsibility, comes the need to make not just one, but a series of decisions that alter the very course of our destiny.

It's easy to understand why we sometimes experience decision paralysis.

Which job do I take? What career do I choose? Do I stay in this relationship? What should I do with my money? Is it time to give up on that friendship? What do I want to do with my business next? Which opportunity is for me?

Whatever the question may be, your purpose is either the answer, or the path to the answer.

In fact, all the answers you will ever need are right there, buried within your calling.

Remember: your purpose is the *reason you are here.*

And thus, the greatest thing you can do for yourself and humanity, is to fulfil that purpose.

This means that every decision you make – from the daily to the destiny-defining – can be made in context of this. You can shape and direct your Earthly life around your soul's purpose.

Remembering this eases the decision-making process, even when it comes to the BIG questions.

With your higher purpose in mind, you can choose the option that aligns most closely with the direction you want to go; the one that moves and inspires you most. Seeing which degree, job, education, relationship, lifestyle, home situation, mentor, friends, and health habits are right for you, becomes simpler.

Your deep knowing will emerge, and you will *feel* what is for, or not for, you.

Not only will seeing every situation in context of your purpose help you to make decisions, but your purpose will also give you the courage you need to follow through on them.

It will empower you to ask for what you want and to say 'No' to what you don't. It will help you to let go and rise up, because you have places to go and dreams to fulfil.

As you move forward on your path, know this:

Ultimately, you can't mess it up. Your life is a platform for you to play on – to find and express who you are – and the only way you could even come close to 'messing it up' is if you keep your dream locked up inside you.

So, live boldly.

No regrets.

You've got this.

“Definiteness of purpose is the starting point of all achievement.”

W. Clement Stone

17

The Career You Dream Of

The desire to know one's purpose is typically triggered by one of two things: either a rock-bottom moment where the value of life comes into clear focus, or an experience of working in an unfulfilling job and feeling a desire for 'more'.

My life journey included both. My rock-bottom moment unfolded with near-suicidal depression at the age of 19 when I questioned what the point of my life was and, simultaneously, discovered my determination to make my life everything it could be.

As it happened, the second trigger had occurred just months earlier, during the only full-time job I had.

I remember working as an administration assistant, feeling empty and knowing in the depths of my *soul* that I wanted more – and that I was born for it. I ached to use what was within me to make a contribution to the world.

From my heart to yours, I get it: you want to do something you *love* for work.

You want spiritual and financial fulfilment.

I am here to tell you that you can have both. The meaning and money that you dream of *can* go hand-in-hand. You can end the conflict between the need for survival (money) and your innate need for meaning (spirituality).

Your purpose is the key to this, and from my experience, the meaning must come *first*.

You must know what you love to do before you can become creative and find ways to earn a living from it. You must discover your gifts, your interests, your strengths, and your talents before you can begin to share them with others and be paid for it. Money flows from meaning.

Therefore, your purpose is the essential foundation for your dream career. It is the key. It is the centrepiece around which you can be paid to do what inspires you.

A work-life without meaning leads to a life that feels empty. But a work-life where every day and every hour feels like part of a legacy? That is worth striving for.

You can fulfil your career in a dream job or in a business; both are vehicles to express and fulfil your purpose. Some people are born for business, and others find their sweet spot working for a company they believe in. It's up to you to choose which one fits you perfectly.

But once you know, give your whole heart to your path.

Apply yourself. Show people what you are made of. Share what is inside you. Let the world know that you are here, and don't be afraid to *care* deeply about what you do.

All of this is the key to great work – and great work seeds great careers.

"When you stay on purpose and refuse to be discouraged by fear, you align with the infinite self, in which all possibilities exist."

Wayne Dyer

18

The Greatness You Are Made Of

I believe that inside every person is a burning desire to find out what we are made of.

We want to discover our power and explore what is possible when we apply ourselves to our calling. We want to use our gifts to make a difference. We want to experience just how far we can go when we give our dreams our all.

That is the pursuit of human greatness; of the potential we know is innate within us and that we were born to express. This is where self-actualisation happens and dreams come to life.

Your purpose is the fuel to this flame.

It provides you with the reason to live and work wholeheartedly, and the goal to aim for.

As you work on building the life and career you desire, it is inevitable that you will grow.

You will learn new skills, try new things, fail, fall on your face, discover who you're not, meet your limits, break them, break down, break through, try things that don't work, and find things that do.

And in that process, day by day and year by year, you will unleash your *greatness*.

Inspired by the vision of your future, you will do things you never dreamed of. You will face your fears, one by one, and with each achievement, you will realise that you are – and always have been – far greater than you ever thought.

The journey of pursuing your purpose will invite you to expand, over and over, until there is no question left in your mind about whether you have infinite potential at the core of you.

It's what you are made of.

If you have spent your life believing that you are small, fulfilling your purpose will show you how *big* you truly are.

If you have spent your life thinking that you can't, fulfilling your purpose will prove to you that you *can*.

If you have spent your life feeling that you aren't intelligent, fulfilling your purpose will reveal exactly how *brilliant* you are.

And if you have spent your life wondering if you are valuable enough, fulfilling your purpose will make clear to you exactly how and in what way you are *precious*.

No matter where you are standing today, there is so much more available for you in this life, and following your purpose is how you discover it.

It is how you meet yourself and experience all that is possible.

"Be faithful to that which exists inside yourself."

Andre Gide

19

Find Your Confidence & Courage

I want you to imagine that there is a bright light at the very core of you. This glow emanates from your soul. It animates your heart, your mind, and your physical body on Earth. It is your purpose.

When you focus on that glow, the light shines brighter.

This occurs in the moments when you are talking about, immersed in, or doing what you love. You become illuminated by your desire to express what is within you and to pursue what fascinates you.

Your personal confidence is natural in that state, because it is impossible to hide who you are when the light within you shines so brightly.

When you actively and consciously engage with your dharma, you see yourself clearly, you know yourself deeply, and you believe in yourself infinitely.

This gives you the courage to honour your heart and soul and do what you were born to do, even when it makes no logical sense to the outside world.

You no longer require the approval of others, nor do you twist, turn, and bend your life trying to please the people around you. You are far more occupied by the pursuit a lifetime: answering to the divine calling within you.

Understanding and honouring your true self in this way gives you a natural magnetism which attracts all manner of miracles into your life. It will transform your reality, right before your eyes.

The light of your purpose reveals YOU.

But, when you take your attention off the light within you – when you repress what you desire, ignore what your heart is telling you, deny your power, and delay doing what inspires you – the glow within you diminishes, and your personal confidence follows.

You start to compare yourself and your life to others, looking to the outside for clarity and measuring your results up against people around you.

You struggle to know who you are. You lose touch with your innate gifts. You start to feel that you are somehow powerless or invisible.

Your lack of confidence leads you to hide behind others success and settle for a career, relationship, social circle, and life that is far less than you deserve and far less than you are capable of. You suppress your potential and live your life in darkness, instead of basking in the light of your authentic self.

Be who you are.

That's where the self-belief and confidence you seek – and the courage you need for a life of greatness – exists.

"Having a sense of purpose is having a sense of self. A course to plot is a destination to hope for."

Bryant H. McGill

20

Your True Worth

Self-worth is a battle that many people face: the deep-seated worry, concern, or feeling that they are somehow worthless or worth-less. The recurring thought that who they are doesn't matter. That underlying belief that what they do in life is of little significance.

The presence and pursuit of your purpose is the antidote to this pain and problem.

It is impossible to do what you love without loving yourself in that moment. In fact, your self-love is likely to be at its greatest in times when you have found yourself in your calling.

In those moments, your heart is online, your mind is focused, and your entire being is consumed by the mastery of what lies before you.

You are fuelled by love.

You are determined, ambitious, and devoted. You are magic in motion, genius at work, creativity unfolding, light working. You feel connected with the universe at large.

It is then that you experience yourself at your most valuable because you are *expressing* the value within you. Your worth is never in question.

When you do what you love, you feel complete – because you *are*. The love for what you are doing touches every single part of your being, from the top of your head to the tips of your toes.

You wouldn't change a thing about yourself. You *love* you.

Any state other than this is a lesser truth; a lie about who you are. Those feelings that you aren't good enough, or that you should somehow be different in order to be significant or loved aren't real.

The same goes for any remark that anyone has written or said about or to you regarding your worth – or rather, a lack of it. If you have ever been told that you are worthless, it isn't true.

The only thing that matters is what resides within you and how you share that with the world around you, for yourself and for humanity.

The more time you spend doing what you love, the greater your comprehension of your true worth will be, especially as you become living proof that it is possible to devote your life to your purpose and fulfil your wildest dreams in the process.

You were born whole and magnificent – and you are *perfect* for your path.

So, please remember this:

You don't need to be *more* than what you are because what you are is *more than enough.*

"Life is never made unbearable by circumstances, but only by lack of meaning and purpose."

Viktor Frankl

21
When It All Falls Apart

It is inevitable: you will face challenges in life.

From relationship breakdowns to career meltdowns to physical issues and financial distress, you will be trialled and tested on your journey.

The difference between letting those adversities break you or make you is how quickly you remember your purpose in the moments when the fire is the hottest and the days are the darkest.

Are you going to believe that nothing works out for you and let this challenge get the better of you? Or are you going to remember why you are truly here and let the truth of that guide you to overcome this seemingly insurmountable obstacle?

Your purpose is *the* reason to rise again, no matter how extreme the defeat.

It is your connection to your highest self: the part of you that is far greater than anything you can face on planet Earth. Therefore, it is the source of all you need to transcend adversity, regardless of what the trial or dilemma may be.

You could be beaten down, exhausted, bleeding on the floor, and still the light of what you were born to do – the real reason you are here – can shine through.

Your purpose inspires you to pull it together, to pull yourself up, and to find healing where there seems to be none. To see the light at the end of the tunnel and the blessing amidst the storm.

You will find the way forwards – because you must. You will draw on strength from the deepest parts of you to keep moving – because there is a reason big enough to keep going. And you won't give up – because giving up is simply not an option.

You will stop at nothing and let nothing stop you on the path of living your dreams.

That's what purpose does.

It gives you the desire to transform yourself in the pursuit of something greater. It gives you the ability to see whatever is happening today as part of the divine plan for your life. It ignites the resilience and power of the human spirit, even when faced with extreme challenge.

That's what your purpose will do for you: guide, nudge, call, and pull you through every twist and turn of your journey and fill you with persistence when the road gets rough.

Your purpose holds greater possibilities for you in its path: greater horizons, greener pastures, richer experiences, a more fulfilling existence.

No obstacle, even those that exist within you, can ever extinguish the fire and spirit in your soul.

“You must first be who you really are, then do what you need to do, in order to have what you want.”

Margaret Young

22

The One Who Stands Beside You

To love and be loved is one of our greatest desires as human beings.

We want to be accepted, understood, cared for, acknowledged, seen, heard, validated, valued, and appreciated for who we are. But how do we balance this with our equally strong desire to fulfil our dharma on planet Earth?

It doesn't have to be an extreme, where we must sacrifice one for the other. It *is* possible to experience both, for these two extraordinary loves to co-exist... and you deserve that.

The essential thing to understand is this: trying to find a partner to fulfil you because your own life feels empty is futile.

Why? Because ultimately, it will lead you right back to where you started: needing to develop the relationship with yourself and figure out what *you* truly want.

The great irony I've always found with romantic relationships, is that the moment you are present and focused on doing what you love – when you are in love with your life and life itself – the next perfect partner suddenly appears, seemingly out of nowhere. It's like a cosmic comedy, that when you love where and who you are, you often manifest a significant other to revel in it with you.

When you devote yourself to building a life around what you love, you send a different frequency out into the world.

You show up as *you*: unashamedly, freely, and without hesitation.

You are authentic, doing what you feel moved to do, and fulfilling your destiny.

And *that* is what attracts the partner who complements you.

The partner who enhances your purpose, rather than pulls you away from it. The partner who stands by your side and who walks with you as you become all you can be and achieve what you are capable of.

The partner who celebrates your wins as you celebrate theirs. The partner who loves you unconditionally – for who you are in your truest essence and all of your expressions – and whose presence enhances your very experience of life.

That relationship is meaningful, where you are in this life together as a team.

There is no sacrifice of self in that partnership. No one has to give up what matters to them for the relationship to 'work' or for the other person to succeed. It's about thriving together, as the people you were destined to be.

The first devotion for you as individuals is your own purpose.

The relationship is then something you share in as you realise your dreams.

That's where the deepest love exists.

Heart-opening, soul-touching, tear-jerking love that awakens your greatness and reminds you every single day just how extraordinary and exquisite you truly are.

“Having a purpose is the difference between making a living and making a life.”

Thomas Thiss

23

Money and Your Purpose

Mastering money is essential if you want to thrive.

Without money, we burn out, stress out, and give up on what matters to us. The cost of ignoring our need and desire for financial wealth is immense.

But when our income and wealth building is on track – and we are in *flow* with money – it transforms our entire experience of life. It brings out the best of who we are.

This is why it matters greatly that we align our financial pursuits to our highest purpose.

Do you need a clear vision for your financial future? Yes. Is it important to make sure your income and investing goals inspire you? Definitely. Will you need to stretch yourself and learn new skills, like managing money, taxes, and wealth creation? Absolutely.

Living on purpose is what will give you the drive and the self-worth to do all the above.

Maybe you won't start out placing a high importance on making and mastering money. But as you start to work on your goals, you *will* realise how essential having financial resources is when it comes to living an extraordinary life.

You will need money to start your business, fund your projects, work with new mentors, build a team, get support, and educate yourself, every single one of which will be a valuable investment into the future you want.

And *this* will require you to let go of any long-standing and limiting paradigms you've held onto around money: that it's evil, that wanting it is greedy, that it's hard to come by, that you don't deserve it, that the world would be a better place without it.

The desire to *use* money for an ultimate purpose – for *your* purpose – will be the incentive you need to transform your relationship with it so that you can experience and build wealth.

So, see money for what it really is: a form of payment in exchange for value.

Then, build a new relationship with money: one where you feel love, respect, and appreciation for it because it enhances your ability to make your vision manifest. Because it enables you to do, achieve, and experience what you desire.

Remember: it is the pursuit of something higher – your dharma, your end-in-mind, the big picture vision for your life – that gives money its *true* meaning.

It is in context of your soul's purpose where you figure out what money means to you and why mastering your financial destiny matters so greatly.

"The best way to lengthen out our days is to walk steadily and with a purpose."

Charles Dickens

24

Unlock Your Longevity & Wellness

Your physical body is one of the greatest gifts you have been given.

It is your home on Earth. It is with you from conception to your passing, and without it, you literally wouldn't be here.

Your body makes every single moment of your life possible.

To experience that life to the fullest – to feel alive and alert and inspired and fulfilled – your body needs to perform optimally. It is the Ferrari to your racetrack, the key to your palace, the foundation for your skyscraper.

It needs an ideal combination of ingredients to flourish: the right nutrients, movement, water, rest, sunshine, food, fluids, treatments.

These are all forms of physical nourishment that enable it to function the way it was designed to; that enable you to look, feel, and move the way you would love.

But your body also needs another kind of nourishment that is *critical* to your wellness.

It needs spiritual nourishment.

Put simply, it needs you to fulfil your purpose.

Doing this brings a type of light, energy, and healing to your body that is unparalleled from any physical supplement or treatment I have experienced. It gives you a direct connection with the very source that animated your life on Earth to begin with.

That higher energy flows from your soul to your heart, through your mind, and illuminates your physical body. It ignites you, and enables you to create, invent, achieve, and succeed.

Your body is your ultimate teammate on the journey of creating and living an extraordinary life. In some ways – and this brings tears to my eyes – your body is your ultimate servant.

It is here, so that *you* can be here.

It breathes, so that *you* can breathe life into your vision.

It moves, so that *you* can move forward with your plans.

It *loves* you, and it wants the same thing that I want for you, that your heart wants for you, that your soul wants for you: for you to *thrive* while sharing your gifts and making your impact.

Your purpose *is* the reason to nourish your body.

So, give it the love and care it is asking for. Listen to its nudges and needs. Honour it.

Remember that it doesn't give up on you, even if you do.

Live fully. Breathe deeply. Move freely.

Be you.

"The heart of human excellence often begins to beat when you discover a pursuit that absorbs you, frees you, challenges you, or gives you a sense of meaning."

Terry Orlick

25

The Calling For Self-Mastery

Fulfilling your purpose requires self-mastery. In fact, pursuing your calling is a daily invitation to grow up into who you are: to master your 'self'.

What is self-mastery?

Self-mastery is the strength to direct your life from within, rather than being influenced by the opinions and desires of others. It is to use your talents, your voice, and your message to serve humanity. It is to be true to yourself, above all else, despite criticism, rejection, fear, and doubt.

It will require you to step up continually, into the greater version of yourself, while simultaneously letting go of behaviours, relationships, dynamics, emotions, wounds, drama, and patterns that you *know* no longer serve you.

I will admit it freely: the journey of self-mastery isn't always easy.

Seeing your own blind spots, being willing to feel the pain in order to heal it, and having the kahunas to reflect inwardly before you blame anyone for *anything*, takes courage.

It takes courage to walk away from situations that don't serve you so that you can pursue bigger opportunities. It takes self-belief to let go of what (and who) no longer works because you want something more for yourself. And it takes devotion to give up any notion that you are or have been, in any way, wounded by the events that have occurred in your life.

All of the above takes vulnerability, humility, patience, and perseverance.

But it *is* rewarding.

Pursuing your purpose is the greatest self-growth path of all, and it holds rewards so big, so deep, so meaningful, and so beautiful that you will want more.

So, lean in.

Listen to the calling within you that wants to guide you to master your life.

Open up, let go, and find yourself. Act courageously. Trust your inner knowing. Believe in who you are. Get busy doing your life's work.

Then, do it again tomorrow.

I never dreamed that I could do what I am doing now when I first started out. It is the path of self-mastery – the path of my purpose – that led me here.

Greater things are waiting for you.

Go find them.

"There's a divine presence, a divine order, in the universe that few people ever get to know. But those who do, their lives are changed forever."

Leibniz

26

THE GOD THAT GUIDES YOUR PATH

Regardless of how you define 'God' or whether you believe in one, it is difficult to question that there is an intelligence greater than us in this universe.

As human beings, we are *tiny*: infinitesimal specks living on a minute planet flying through space. Our entire existence on Earth is governed by that greater intelligence, the source, the higher order.

When you open your mind and heart to that intelligence, your life takes on a whole new level of magic and meaning. In fact, the experience is often so profound that it is tear-jerking. Life-changing.

You experience a deep sense of belonging. You *know* that you are meant to be here, and you *know* to your core that every moment of your time here is guided by that higher force.

This deep knowing gives you the faith you need to take the next step, the belief you need in yourself, and the perseverance you need to succeed. Why? Because you realise that you cannot fail, only grow, and that you are never alone.

Your purpose is your most direct line of connection to this experience: to a 'God experience' of life.

When you give your whole heart to your purpose in life, you stand with God. Because you are doing what God designed for you to do.

You are at your most authentic. You experience an ultimate oneness with your perfection, and thus, the divine perfection that flows through every level of this entire universe.

You become the most connected to yourself – to the infinite world within you – and this opens the channel to feel simultaneously connected to the infinite world around you.

It takes courage, for sure, to honour your calling and the vision inside your heart with religious devotion. But every time you answer the call, you will be right there.

Shoulder-to-shoulder and deeply connected with the force that created you. The force that wants you to shine; to make the most of your existence, to squeeze every drop out of your life, to live wholeheartedly.

To serve God in this way is to the ultimate service to yourself, and to serve yourself in this way is the ultimate service to God. It is for you to fully participate in and accept, enjoy, and grow into your unique and significant role in this universe.

Life and all of its events – including your very birth – are not random. They are part of a greater plan unfolding. An extraordinary destiny in motion. A higher purpose manifesting.

And when you live fully into your own higher purpose, you will become consciously aware of it. Aware of the perfection that creates, values, and believes in you in every single moment of your life.

"What I am living for and what I am dying for are the same question."

Margaret Atwood

27

You Can Be An Inspiration

People who do and achieve extraordinary things become leaders in the world.

Their success shows others just how much is possible,

Their tenacity demonstrates just how resilient, resourceful, and talented human beings are,

And their accomplishments raise the bar for those around them.

By fulfilling their dreams, they ignite that same spark in all the people whose lives they touch: the spark of purpose.

By being who they are and doing what they love, they give other people permission to cast their fears aside and walk the road less travelled. To live an original, authentic life.

You have this same power and potential within you. The way you choose to live your life *can* light the path for others.

By following your heart and creating a career around your purpose, you can become living proof that great dreams give rise to great achievement.

You can make an impact, change lives, and teach others through your very presence, that we are *not* put here on Earth to struggle, but rather to *thrive*.

You can show people that it is in the courage to live boldly that we find the greatest rewards in life. Your presence and results can encourage them to excel.

That is true leadership: when who you *are* is an inspiration to those around you.

I truly believe that my life on Earth is my message for humanity, just as much as my writings themselves. I wish for my path to remind others of their own, and for the dreams I fulfil to inspire others to fulfil their heartfelt visions.

Remembering that I also live to set an example for people who need hope, pulls me through on the toughest of my days. When I feel down and out or I am absorbed with self-doubt and struggle, I remind myself that every action I take matters greatly and that what I do, *counts*. As they say, you never know who is watching.

What kind of influence do you want to have on others? What message do you want your life to send to the people you meet?

I am sure that you, too, want to be someone who awakens the spirit inside those they care about: children, partner, family, friends, community, customers, team, nation, the world.

You were born for this.

To take the stage and lead.

To light the pathway for those in darkness.

"Lean forward into your life. Live each day as if it were on purpose."

Mary Anne Radmacher

28

Fulfil Your Destiny On Earth

Once you know what your life is truly about, how do you fulfil your destiny on Earth?

First, understand that it is not an overnight process. It is a journey with many, many destinations along the way.

Where you are now is already a long way from where you started, and where you will be in one, five, or ten years will be drastically different to where you stand today.

You will meet successes, failures, victory, doubt, obstacles, and milestones as you focus on achieving the next level of what you want to do here – just as you have already done to reach this point. They are all part of the extraordinary ride and story of your life.

There is no point at which you will have finally "made it", because then you will be fuelled by the next idea, vision, goal, or project that inspires you.

My advice is to remember that each moment of your journey is just as precious as any other. It is all part of you being and becoming who you are, so *enjoy* it.

Your life is far more precious than you can comprehend right now, and time *will* pass by quicker than you realise.

So, make the most of every single second of it.

Do what you love. Balance what you need to do today with what you want to do tomorrow. Work on your plans for the future as much as you work on your present-day responsibilities. Push distractions away so that you can focus on what matters most. Close the gap between the life you live today and the life you dream of.

Be courageous in overcoming your obstacles and resilient in the face of challenge. Stand up for what matters. Pay attention to the signs from around you, the messages within you, and the visions that move you.

Live your life with the deep *trust* that you will always have what you need, right when you need it, to take the next step.

Trust that the right person, the right idea, the right education, the right piece of information, and the right opportunity will manifest. Trust that you will be in the right place at the right time to meet the next success, and that you will be *ready* when it happens.

Never stop working on your craft: whether that is dancing, researching, writing, singing, cooking, bodybuilding, teaching, or healing.

Give yourself wholly to what lies within your soul.

Follow your heart to the ends of the Earth if it calls you to.

Do what you were born to do.

Give yourself the life you want.

Live extraordinary.

"You were put on this Earth to achieve your greatest self, to live out your purpose, and to do it courageously."

Dr Steve Maraboli

29

The Pauses Along The Way

There may come moments on your journey where you feel burned out: deeply exhausted, drained, and empty, with nothing left to give.

Days where you have given it all and done all that you can to reach a goal.

Times when you can't think or see clearly, and where you have nothing left in your tank.

From my experience, these times are bound to happen when you are living fully towards a vision: when you are pushing yourself to achieve new things, to do what you have never done before, and to unleash even more of what is inside you.

Whether it's from building a business, training your body, caring for others, speaking on stages, producing new work, or serving people, just know this: it is *okay* to rest.

In fact, it is necessary.

I could not write a book about finding and fulfilling your purpose without acknowledging the importance of 'the pause' when pursuing your destiny.

The 'pause' is exactly that: a moment to stop.

It is a moment to let the dust settle so that you can see what to do next.

It is a time to rest, recharge, and reset your entire system: body, mind, and soul.

It is a chance to see how far you have come and to remember why you started.

It is an opportunity to receive the breathing room you need to direct your path of destiny, your life, and your work here.

And it is a moment to turn inwards for advice, to align and realign yourself with what matters.

How you choose to stop and rest is up to you. Only you know what feels best; and what you need to bring yourself back to life.

But what I do know is this:

The vision inside your heart, of what you would love to do and of what you know the world needs, cannot and will not happen without you. It is unique to you – and your purpose *needs* you.

You are the most valuable asset you have.

You are your greatest resource.

And this world *needs* you.

So, take care of yourself.

Look out for yourself as you forge forwards on your path.

"When you were born, you cried and the world rejoiced. Live your life so that when you die, the world cries and you rejoice."

Indian Proverb

30

Your Legacy For Humanity

You are a soul made incarnate into a physical body.

I truly believe that the divine purpose of your life is to allow that soul to express itself wholly and fully in this world, and that every single moment of your journey is beckoning for exactly that.

To let what is within you, out.

To allow what you feel, to flow.

To follow the path of interest until the end.

To create what yearns to be created.

To build what asks to be built.

To say what wants to be said.

To discover what is waiting to be found.

To change what is ready for a breakthrough.

This is how we leave our legacy: by becoming an open channel for the divine source that lives inside us all.

Above all else, we make our greatest impact by honouring and living in alignment with that.

By listening to the whispers that speak inside us, by following through on the ideas that never leave us, and by doing what our heart asks us to pursue.

This is where the purest expression of our potential emerges. It's where and how we fulfil our purpose here.

There will be moments when you stop and look around and behind you to realise that you have left a trail, where people's lives are being enriched by what *you* have said, done, produced, and initiated. That is your legacy.

There will be other moments when your mind is so quiet and your heart is so open, that you see a prophetic vision of what 'could be'. That is also your legacy.

Your legacy is a continual dance between the difference you have already made and that you are yet to make.

You might not know exactly what your legacy is as you sit there today, nor know the bounds of what is possible for your impact on humanity. You may have no idea where this path of destiny will lead you or the difference it will make on the lives of others.

But what I do know is this: YOU and the very life you are living are already leaving your legacy. And you pursuing what is in your heart, to share your God-given gifts, expressing what lives at the very core of your soul?

That is what will make your greatest mark on the human race.

Your legacy is YOU.

"Do not forget who you are and where you come from. You are made of the brightest stars and the widest oceans. You are made of the highest mountains and the tallest trees. You are made of magic and dreams, wishes, and light. You have heroes, warriors, kings, queens, gods, and goddesses flowing through your veins. You come from infinite possibilities and incredible odds. You are here for a reason."

Nikki Banas

Conclusion

Deep inside your heart, you *know* who you are and what you want to do with your life.

You know what brings you meaning, what fascinates you, what you care about, what touches your heart, what moves your soul, what ignites your spirit.

You know what you were brought to this Earth to do.

You just need the courage to admit it and then pursue your calling down every road it takes you.

To let the path you are on *grow* you: to expand who you are, to challenge your old limits, to overturn beliefs about what you are capable of, to heal your emotions, to open you up to your true potential.

That's how great lives are made.

With heartfelt *vision*,

Relentless *persistence*,

Deep-seated *courage*,

And the willingness to *expand*.

Those big leaps that you feel called to take are the ones that open the door to the existence that lights you up, on every level.

So, let your inner sense of what is possible, together with your undying commitment to give yourself the life you deserve, lead you to where you most want to be.

You have no idea just *how much* is possible once you surrender wholeheartedly to your purpose and allow it to guide every moment and every day of your life.

You've got this,

You deserve this,

And you are ready for it.

So...

Lean into your purpose, *fully*.

Even if it requires courage from the deepest part of you – lean in.

Even if it pushes you to let go of being small and insignificant – lean in.

Take the next step, because magnificence is waiting.

A life of purpose is yours.

Acknowledgements

My gratitude extends to Dario Hogg for the meaningful conversation we shared before I started writing this book. The depth of our exchange inspired me and ignited the vision for *Reflections on Purpose*. Thank you.

To my man and partner, Michael Bromley. Thank you for standing by my side and for supporting me endlessly to fulfil my dharma. Your constant love and presence in my life inspires and encourages me to be the woman this universe intended for me to be. Thank you for guiding me to express my purpose and for reminding me of the power of love.

To my gorgeous mother, Mama Rae, where would I be without you? Not only have you given me life, but you have stood by my side in many times that count. Your endless devotion to seeing me thrive humbles me. To say that I feel blessed to have you as my mother is an understatement. You are my best friend, my family, my heart. I love you x

My heartfelt thanks go to Dr John Demartini for further igniting the purpose that lives within me, and for encouraging me to pursue my calling. Your inspiration over the years has reminded me who I am and encouraged me to play a bigger game.

To my dear friend, Dr Marcia Becherel. For more than a decade, you have been by my side as I have pursued the greatest adventure of all: my purpose. You have picked me up when I have stumbled and helped me to reconnect with my inner truth and wisdom in more moments than I can count. Thank you for your friendship and for sharing in a heartfelt exploration of God and the hidden order of life. I love you. You are family.

Thank you to my other mentors, spiritual teachers, and healers who have guided me over the years to connect with my heart and my dreams. I am grateful for each moment where I have been reminded of who I am and what I feel I am here to do.

Thank you to my amazing team at Gowor International Publishing who assisted with the production of this book. I am deeply thankful for your devotion to your work and for your support in my mission.

And finally, thank you to my readers. Thank you for trusting your deep inner knowing that there is more to you – and more to your life on Earth – than first meets the eye. It is my wish that my writings will continue to ignite that spark of purpose inside you, especially during times when life feels most challenging, so that you can continue to express your potential in life. You deserve an amazing existence and great things truly are possible for you.

About The Author

Emily Gowor is an Inspirational Writer, Author & Keynote Speaker.

After overcoming near-suicidal depression, Emily devoted herself and her life to bringing writing and inspiration to the world. She has now spent more than 15 years helping people to live an extraordinary life.

As the author of more than 12 published books on the topics of self-help, entrepreneurship, and writing – including *Born Great* and *The Inspirational Messenger* – Emily produced an award-winning blog, *Life Travels* which attracted thousands of readers. Emily has shared the stage with several influential individuals, including Dr. John Demartini, human behaviour expert, best-selling author and star of *The Secret*.

Emily's writings, projects, and speaking presentations have touched and moved thousands globally as she inspires people to reach for more.

As a winner of the 2012 and 2014 Anthill 30under30 Young Entrepreneur Award, Emily has been featured in a range of media sharing her inspirational messages.

Having already fulfilled upon a profound and thriving career, Emily finds continual inspiration in life as she continues to bring her love for humanity to the forefront into all she does.

For speaking engagements, media, and inquiries, log on to:

www.emilygowor.com

Other Books by Emily Gowor

Born Great is a deeply inspirational book that will encourage you to fulfil your purpose on Earth.

Written in 3 parts – Vision, Wealth & Work – *Born Great* will guide you to create the extraordinary life that you are capable of. Exploring topics from purpose through to our relationship with money and how to turn what you love into a career path, this book will be your companion as you pursue your destiny.

Foreword by Dr John Demartini

Available in Kindle, paperback & hardback

Do you know deep down that you were born to touch the world in a meaningful way?

The Inspirational Messenger shares the 5 pillars to becoming inspirational in everything that you do.

This powerful and heart-opening book was written in just four days, channelled from Emily's heart and soul.

It will remind you who you are and inspire you to share your gifts with humanity.

Available in paperback & Kindle

www.ingramcontent.com/pod-product-compliance
Ingram Content Group UK Ltd.
Pitfield, Milton Keynes, MK11 3LW, UK
UKHW062309290726
14090UKWH00018B/964